Your opinion is important to us,
feel free to leave your opinion on Amazon
because it will help us improve
our future publication.

# LEARN
# ALEF BET
# HEBREW ALPHABET LETTERS
## FOR KIDS AND ADULTS
### Handwritten and Print Type
### BEGINNERS

## THIS BOOK BELONGS TO

-------------------------------------------------------------

-------------------------------------------------------------

# Contents

# LET'S START LEARNING HEBREW ALPHABET

See inside

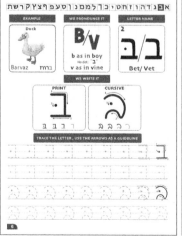

# HEBREW
## Alef Bet

Hebrew is read and written from right to left ⟵

| Vav | Hey | Dalet | Gimmel | Bet/Vet | Alef |
|---|---|---|---|---|---|
| ו | ה | ד | ג | ב | א |
| 6 | 5 | 4 | 3 | 2 | 1 |

| Khaf final | Kaf/Khaf | Yod | Tet | Chet | Zayin |
|---|---|---|---|---|---|
| ך | כ | י | ט | ח | ז |
| 20 | 20 | 10 | 9 | 8 | 7 |

| Semekh | Nun final | Nun | Mem final | Mem | Lamed |
|---|---|---|---|---|---|
| ס | ן | נ | ם | מ | ל |
| 60 | 50 | 50 | 40 | 40 | 30 |

| Qof | Tsade final | Tsade | Fey final | Fey | 'Ayin |
|---|---|---|---|---|---|
| ק | ץ | צ | ף | פ | ע |
| 100 | 90 | 90 | 80 | 80 | 70 |

| Tav | Shin/Sin | Resh |
|---|---|---|
| ת | ש | ר |
| 400 | 300 | 200 |

1

## EXAMPLE

**Rabbit**

Arnav     ארנב

## WE PRONOUNCE IT

Silent letter

## LETTER NAME

**Alef**

## WE WRITE IT

### PRINT

### CURSIVE

## TRACE THE LETTER , USE THE ARROWS AS A GUIDELINE

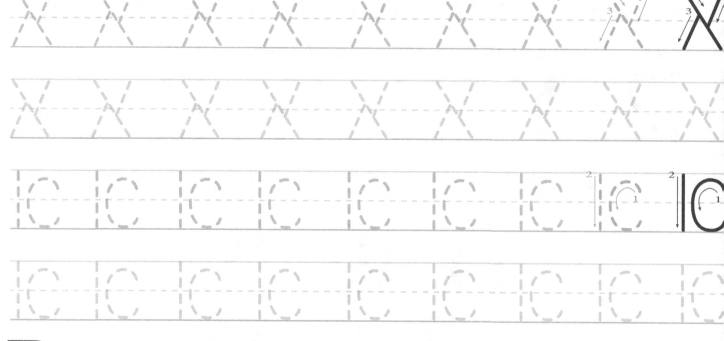

## Cursive Practice

X

**WELL DONE** you have just added a new star to your progress in this book

★☆☆☆☆☆☆☆☆☆☆☆☆☆☆☆☆☆☆☆☆☆☆☆☆

| EXAMPLE | WE PRONOUNCE IT | LETTER NAME |
|---|---|---|

**Duck**

Barvaz ברווז

**B/V**

**b as in boy**

No dot : "ב"

**v as in vine**

2

**ב/ב**

**Bet/ Vet**

## WE WRITE IT

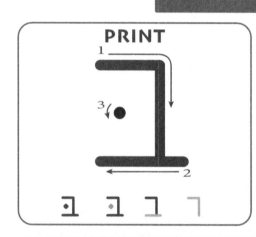

**PRINT**

ב ב ב ר

**CURSIVE**

ב ב ב ר

## TRACE THE LETTER , USE THE ARROWS AS A GUIDELINE

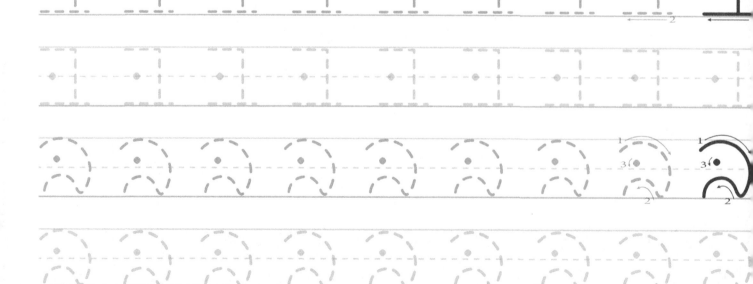

**WELL DONE** you have just added a new star to your progress in this book

★★☆☆☆☆☆☆☆☆☆☆☆☆☆☆☆☆☆☆☆☆☆☆☆☆☆

אבגדהוזחטיכךלמםנסעפפצצקרשת

**EXAMPLE**

Socks

Garbayim  גרביים

**WE PRONOUNCE IT**

g as in girl

**LETTER NAME**

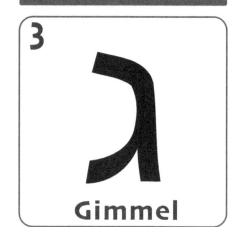

Gimmel

**WE WRITE IT**

PRINT

CURSIVE

**TRACE THE LETTER , USE THE ARROWS AS A GUIDELINE**

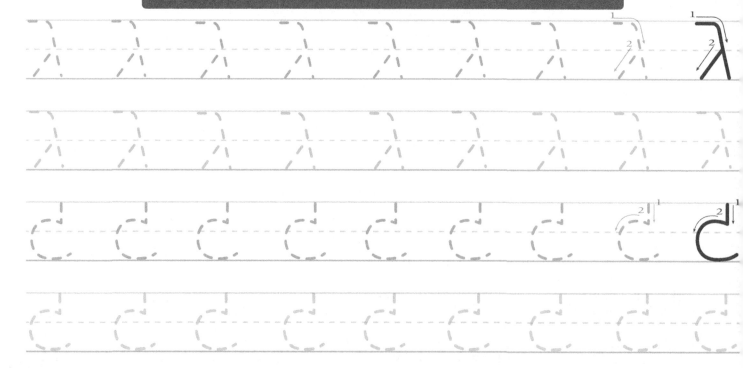

10

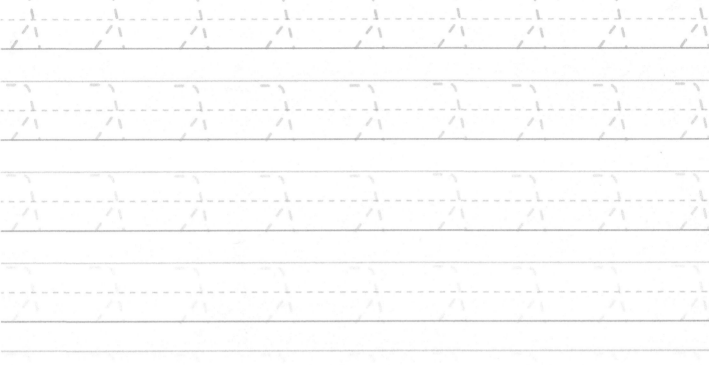

λ

d

א ב ג ד ה ה ו ז ח ט י כ ר ל מ ס נ ו ס ע פ פ צ צ ק ר ש ת

## EXAMPLE

Dinosaur

Dinozaur דינוזאור

## WE PRONOUNCE IT

d as in door

## LETTER NAME

4

Dalet

## WE WRITE IT

PRINT

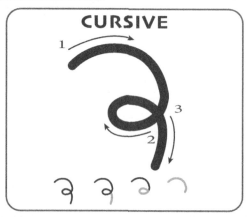

CURSIVE

## TRACE THE LETTER , USE THE ARROWS AS A GUIDELINE

14

## Cursive Practice

T

**WELL DONE** you have just added a new star to your progress in this book

★★★★☆☆☆☆☆☆☆☆☆☆☆☆☆☆☆☆☆☆☆☆☆☆☆

## EXAMPLE

Mountain

Har        הר

## WE PRONOUNCE IT

h as in hay

## LETTER NAME

5

Hey

## WE WRITE IT

### PRINT

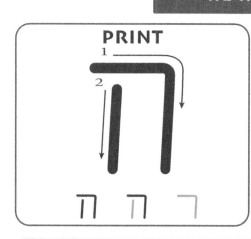

### CURSIVE

## TRACE THE LETTER , USE THE ARROWS AS A GUIDELINE

꼬

**WELL DONE** you have just added a new star to your progress in this book

★★★★★☆☆☆☆☆☆☆☆☆☆☆☆☆☆☆☆☆☆☆

## EXAMPLE

Viconia

Vkinya　　ויקוניה

## WE PRONOUNCE IT

v as in vine

## LETTER NAME

Vav

## WE WRITE IT

### PRINT

### CURSIVE

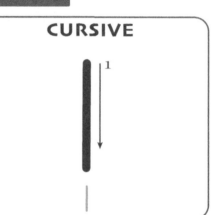

## TRACE THE LETTER , USE THE ARROWS AS A GUIDELINE

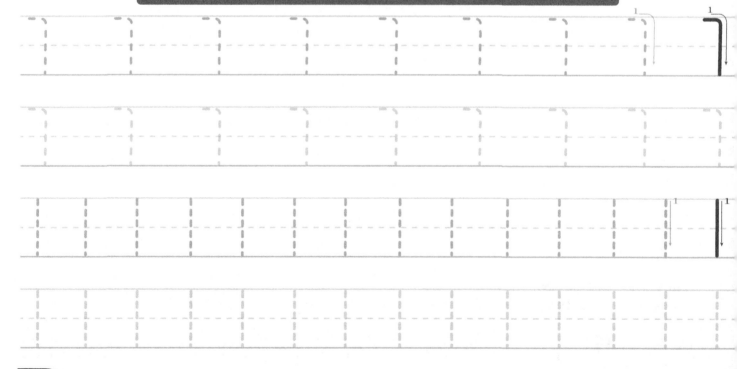

Cursive Practice

**WELL DONE** you have just added a new star to your progress in this book

★★★★★★☆☆☆☆☆☆☆☆☆☆☆☆☆☆☆☆☆☆☆☆☆

| EXAMPLE | WE PRONOUNCE IT | LETTER NAME |
|---|---|---|

**Wolf**

Zehev      זאב

**z as in zebra**

6

**Zayin**

## WE WRITE IT

| PRINT | CURSIVE |
|---|---|

### TRACE THE LETTER , USE THE ARROWS AS A GUIDELINE

27

5

**WELL DONE** you have just added a new star to your progress in this book

★★★★★★★⭐︎☆☆☆☆☆☆☆☆☆☆☆☆☆☆☆☆☆☆☆☆☆

| EXAMPLE | WE PRONOUNCE IT | LETTER NAME |
|---|---|---|

**Milk**

Chalav חלב

## ch

**ch as in Bach**

**8**

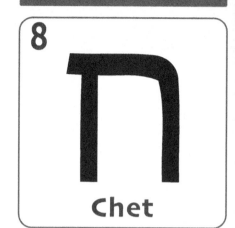

**Chet**

### WE WRITE IT

| PRINT | CURSIVE |
|---|---|

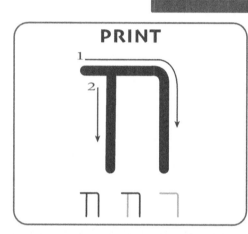

### TRACE THE LETTER , USE THE ARROWS AS A GUIDELINE

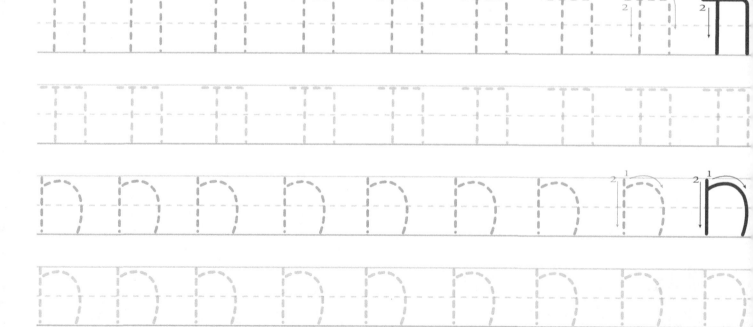

Cursive Practice

ᄁ

h

## EXAMPLE

### Peacock

Tavass    טווס

## WE PRONOUNCE IT

# T

**t as in time**

## LETTER NAME

9

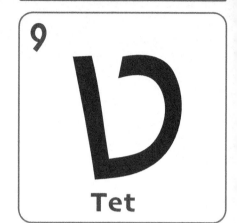

**Tet**

## WE WRITE IT

### PRINT

### CURSIVE

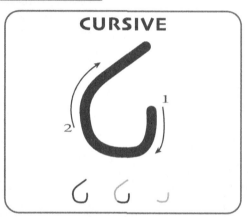

## TRACE THE LETTER , USE THE ARROWS AS A GUIDELINE

4 4 4 4 4 4 4 4 4 4

4 4 4 4 4 4 4 4 4 4

4 4 4 4 4 4 4 4 4

4

6 6 6 6 6 6 6 6 6 6

6 6 6 6 6 6 6 6 6 6

6 6 6 6 6 6 6 6

6 6 6 6 6 6

| EXAMPLE | WE PRONOUNCE IT | LETTER NAME |
|---|---|---|

**Owl**

Yanshuf ינשוף

**y as in yes**

"consonantal vowel"

**10**

**Yod**

## WE WRITE IT

| PRINT | CURSIVE |
|---|---|

## TRACE THE LETTER , USE THE ARROWS AS A GUIDELINE

Cursive Practice

7

| EXAMPLE | WE PRONOUNCE IT | LETTER NAME |
|---|---|---|

**Hat**

Kova      כובע

# K/KH

### k as in kite
No dot : "כ"
## ch as in bach

**20**

## כ/ב

## Kaf/Khaf

## WE WRITE IT

**PRINT**

כ כ כ ר

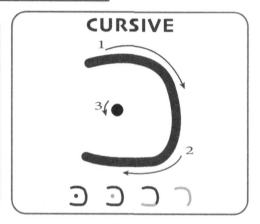

**CURSIVE**

כ כ כ ר

## TRACE THE LETTER , USE THE ARROWS AS A GUIDELINE

**WELL DONE** you have just added a new star to your progress in this book

★★★★★★★★★★★★★☆☆☆☆☆☆☆☆☆☆☆☆☆☆☆☆☆

| Example of word ending with khaf sofit | WE PRONOUNCE IT | LETTER NAME |
|---|---|---|

### King

Melech     מלך

## Sofit form

**20**

## Khaf Final

## WE WRITE IT

| PRINT | CURSIVE |
|---|---|

## TRACE THE LETTER , USE THE ARROWS AS A GUIDELINE

**Cursive Practice**

T

| EXAMPLE | WE PRONOUNCE IT | LETTER NAME |
|---|---|---|

Lizard

Letah    לטאה

**L**

l as in look

30

**Lamed**

## WE WRITE IT

PRINT

CURSIVE

## TRACE THE LETTER , USE THE ARROWS AS A GUIDELINE

7

## EXAMPLE

Coat

Me'il     מעיל

## WE PRONOUNCE IT

**M**

m as in mom

## LETTER NAME

40

**מ**

Mem

## WE WRITE IT

### PRINT

### CURSIVE

## TRACE THE LETTER , USE THE ARROWS AS A GUIDELINE

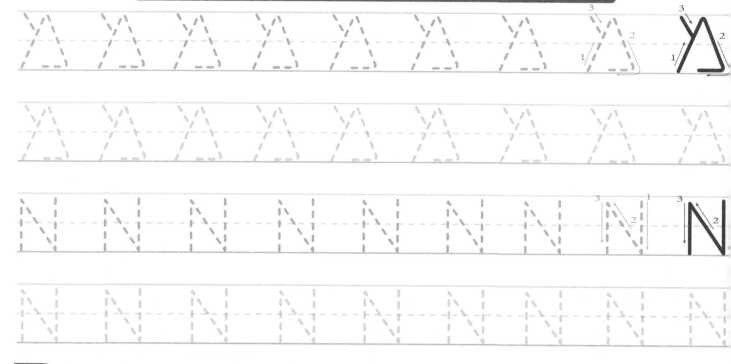

## Cursive Practice

**WELL DONE** you have just added a new star to your progress in this book

★★★★★★★★★★★★★★★★★☆☆☆☆☆☆☆☆☆☆☆☆☆☆☆

| Example of word ending with Mem sofit | WE PRONOUNCE IT | LETTER NAME |
|---|---|---|
| **Kettle**  Kumkum  קומקום | **Sofit form** | 40 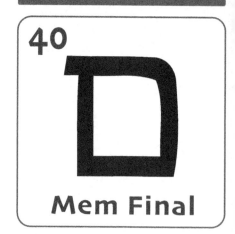 **Mem Final** |

## WE WRITE IT

| PRINT | CURSIVE |
|---|---|
| 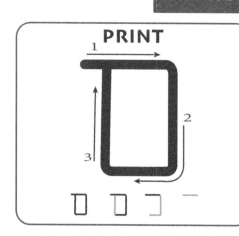 |  |

## TRACE THE LETTER , USE THE ARROWS AS A GUIDELINE

Cursive Practice

$\rho$

**WELL DONE** you have just added a new star to your progress in this book

★★★★★★★★★★★★★★★★★☆☆☆☆☆☆☆☆☆☆☆☆

## EXAMPLE

**Ant**

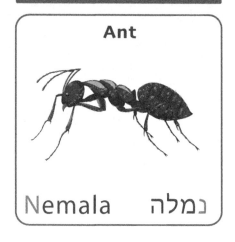

Nemala נמלה

## WE PRONOUNCE IT

**N**

**n as in now**

## LETTER NAME

50

**Nun**

## WE WRITE IT

### PRINT

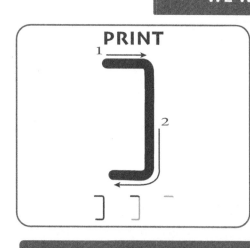

### CURSIVE

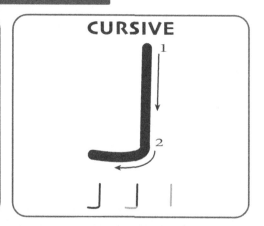

## TRACE THE LETTER , USE THE ARROWS AS A GUIDELINE

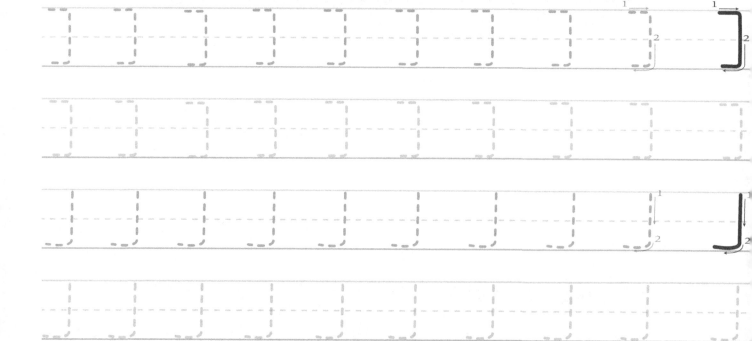

63

**WELL DONE** you have just added a new star to your progress in this book

★★★★★★★★★★★★★★★★★★★★★☆☆☆☆☆☆☆☆☆☆☆☆

| Example of word ending with Nun sofit | WE PRONOUNCE IT | LETTER NAME |
|---|---|---|

### Gardener

Ganan     גנן

### Sofit form

**50**

## Nun Final

---

## WE WRITE IT

| PRINT | CURSIVE |
|---|---|

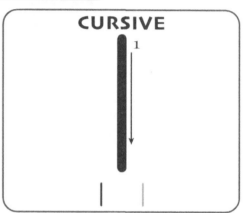

---

## TRACE THE LETTER , USE THE ARROWS AS A GUIDELINE

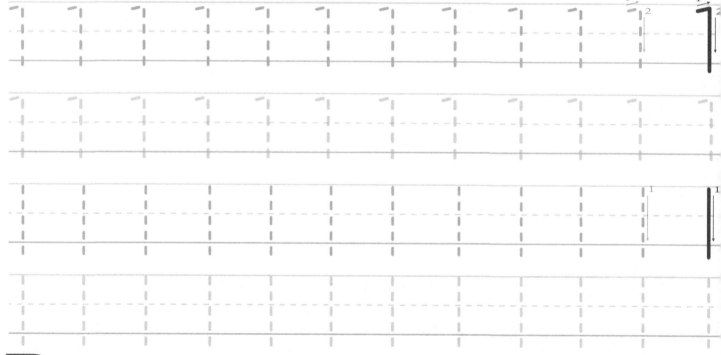

67

1

## EXAMPLE

Knife

Sakkin     סכין

## WE PRONOUNCE IT

**S**

s as in son

## LETTER NAME

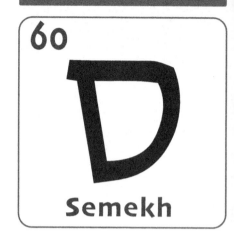

60

**Semekh**

## WE WRITE IT

### PRINT

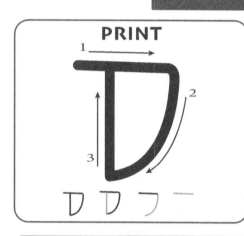

### CURSIVE

## TRACE THE LETTER , USE THE ARROWS AS A GUIDELINE

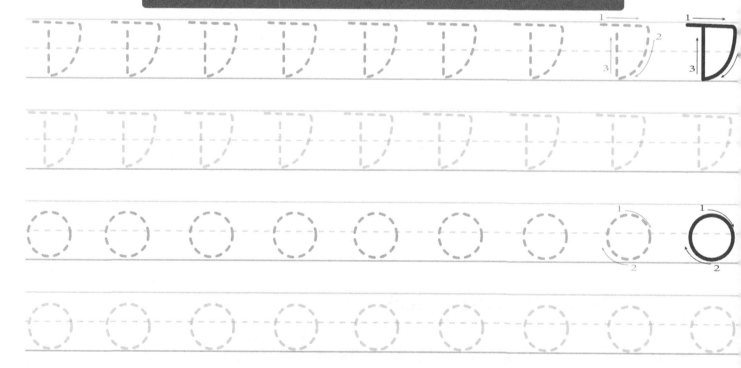

**Cursive Practice**

D

**WELL DONE** you have just added a new star to your progress in this book

★★★★★★★★★★★★★★★★★★★★★☆☆☆☆☆☆☆☆☆☆☆

## EXAMPLE

**Grapes**

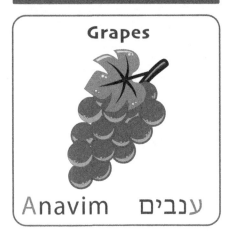

Anavim    ענבים

## WE PRONOUNCE IT

**Silent letter**

## LETTER NAME

70

ʻAyin

## WE WRITE IT

### PRINT

### CURSIVE

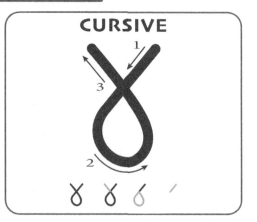

## TRACE THE LETTER , USE THE ARROWS AS A GUIDELINE

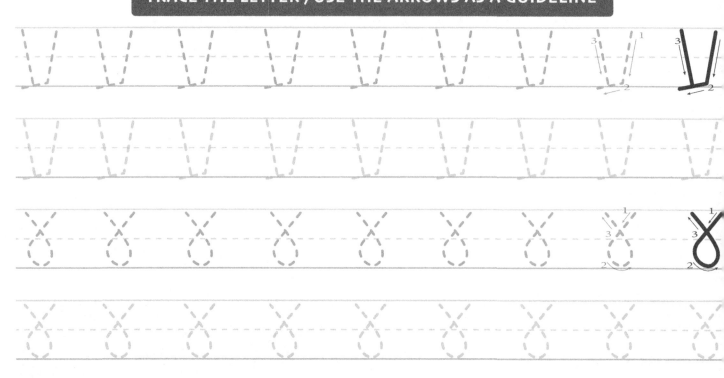

Cursive Practice

V

| EXAMPLE | WE PRONOUNCE IT | LETTER NAME |
|---|---|---|

**Pasta**

Pastah     פסטה

**P/F**

p as in park

No dot (f/ ph) "פ"

**ph as in phone**

80

**Pey/Fey**

## WE WRITE IT

| PRINT | CURSIVE |
|---|---|

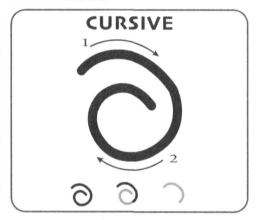

## TRACE THE LETTER , USE THE ARROWS AS A GUIDELINE

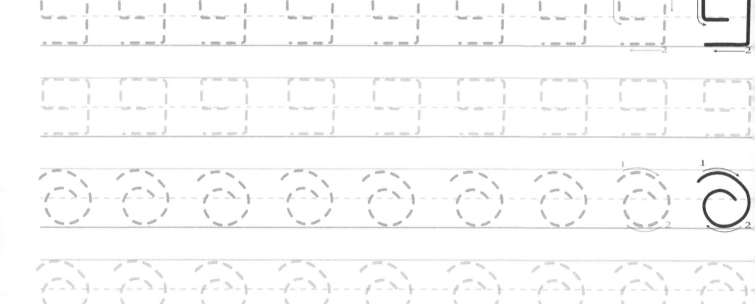

⅃

**WELL DONE** you have just added a new star to your progress in this book

| Example of word ending with Fey sofit | WE PRONOUNCE IT | LETTER NAME |
|---|---|---|

**Rhino**

Karnaf קרנף

Sofit form

80

**Fey Final**

## WE WRITE IT

**PRINT**

**CURSIVE**

## TRACE THE LETTER , USE THE ARROWS AS A GUIDELINE

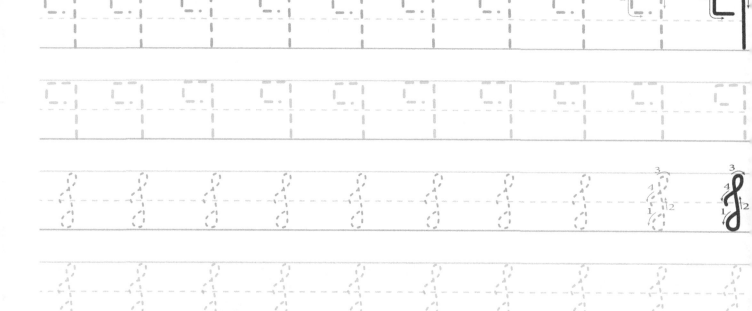

82

Cursive Practice

ᑫ

**WELL DONE** you have just added a new star to your progress in this book

★★★★★★★★★★★★★★★★★★★★★★★☆☆☆☆☆☆

## EXAMPLE

**Scarf**

Tza'if     צעיף

## WE PRONOUNCE IT

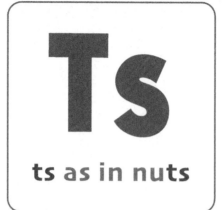

**Ts**

ts as in nuts

## LETTER NAME

90

**Tsade**

## WE WRITE IT

### PRINT

### CURSIVE

---

## TRACE THE LETTER , USE THE ARROWS AS A GUIDELINE

**Cursive Practice**

Y

**WELL DONE** you have just added a new star to your progress in this book

★★★★★★★★★★★★★★★★★★★★★★★★★☆☆☆☆☆☆

## Example of word ending with Tsade sofit

Iron

Maghezz מגהץ

## WE PRONOUNCE IT

Sofit form

## LETTER NAME

90

Tsade Final

## WE WRITE IT

### PRINT

### CURSIVE

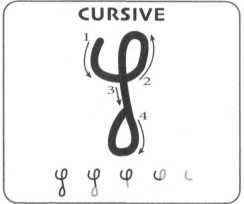

## TRACE THE LETTER , USE THE ARROWS AS A GUIDELINE

Y

| EXAMPLE | WE PRONOUNCE IT | LETTER NAME |
|---|---|---|

Kangaroo

Kengeru     קנגרו

q as in queen

100

Qof

## WE WRITE IT

PRINT

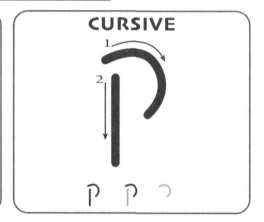

CURSIVE

## TRACE THE LETTER , USE THE ARROWS AS A GUIDELINE

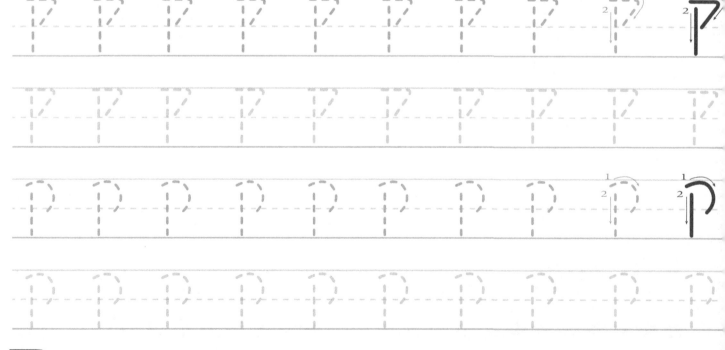

P

**WELL DONE** you have just added a new star to your progress in this book

★★★★★★★★★★★★★★★★★★★★★★★★☆☆☆

## EXAMPLE

**Raccoon**

Rakun       רקון

## WE PRONOUNCE IT

**r as in rain**

## LETTER NAME

**200**

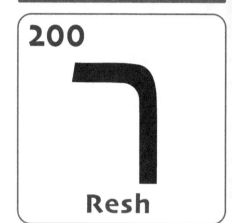

**Resh**

## WE WRITE IT

### PRINT

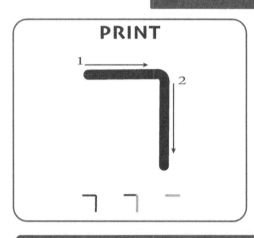

### CURSIVE

## TRACE THE LETTER , USE THE ARROWS AS A GUIDELINE

**Cursive Practice**

**WELL DONE** you have just added a new star to your progress in this book

★★★★★★★★★★★★★★★★★★★★★★★★★★★★★★★★★☆☆

| EXAMPLE | WE PRONOUNCE IT | LETTER NAME |
|---|---|---|

### EXAMPLE

**Clock**

Sha'on     שעון

### WE PRONOUNCE IT

**sh/s**

dot on the Right: "שׁ"
**sh as in shy**

dot on the Left: "שׂ"
**s as in sun**

### LETTER NAME

300

ש/שׂ

**Shin/Sin**

## WE WRITE IT

**PRINT**

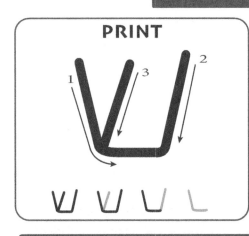

**CURSIVE**

## TRACE THE LETTER , USE THE ARROWS AS A GUIDELINE

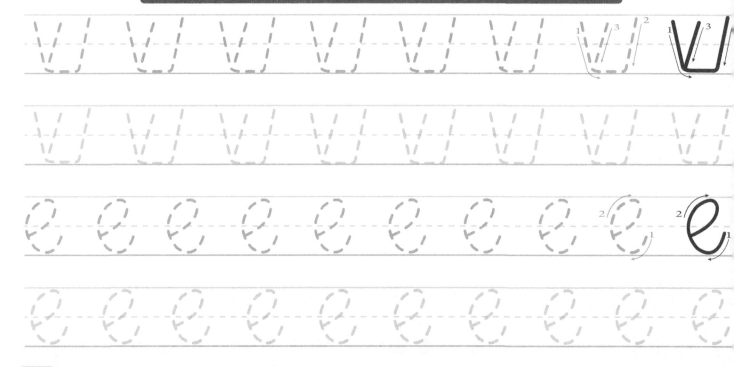

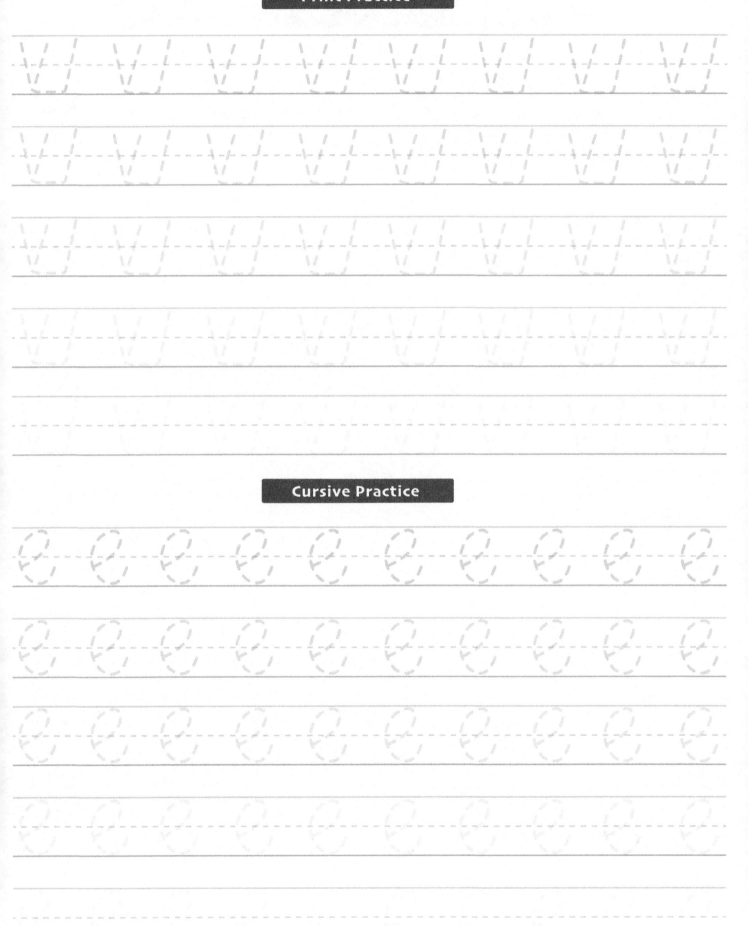

W

*e*

**WELL DONE** you have just added a new star to your progress in this book

★★★★★★★★★★★★★★★★★★★★★★★★★★★★★★★☆

| EXAMPLE | WE PRONOUNCE IT | LETTER NAME |
|---------|-----------------|-------------|

Octopus

Tamnon    תמנון

**T**

**t as in tall**

400

ת

**Tav**

## WE WRITE IT

| PRINT | CURSIVE |
|-------|---------|

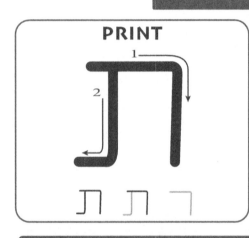

## TRACE THE LETTER , USE THE ARROWS AS A GUIDELINE

Л

**WELL DONE** you have just added a new star to your progress in this book

★★★★★★★★★★★★★★★★★★★★★★★★★★★★★★★★

# The Hebrew vowels

The Symbol " ⊙ " Represents whatever
Hebrew letter is used

**VOWELS**

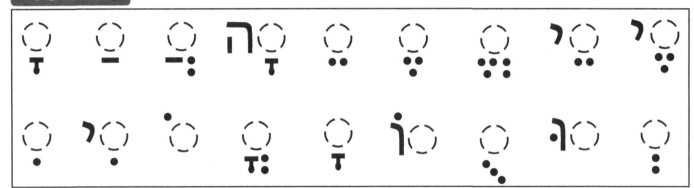

The vowels can be simply classified into
these Five sounds ( A,E,I,O,U )

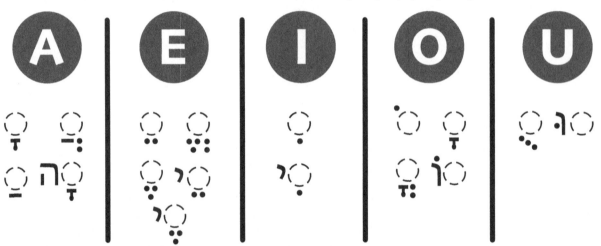

| | The "A" class vowels | | | |
|---|---|---|---|---|
| **Mark** | **Name Vowel** | **Sound** | **Trans.** | **Class** |
| ⊙ָ | Qamets | "a" as in car | a | Long |
| ⊙ַ | Patach | "a" as in hut | a | Short |
| ⊙ֲ | Chateph patach | "a" as in utterly | a | Reduced |
| הֹ⊙ָ | Qamets Hey | "a" as in far | ah | Long |

## The "E" class vowels

| Mark | Name Vowel | Sound | Trans. | Class |
|---|---|---|---|---|
| ◌ | Tsere | "ei" as in eight<br>"e" as in they | ei/e | Long |
| ◌ | Segol | "e" as in bed | e | Short |
| ◌ | Chateph Segol | "e" as in bed | e | Reduced |
| ◌ | Tsere Yod | "ei" as in eight | ei | Long |
| ◌ | Segol Yod | "ey" as in obey | ey | Long |

## The "I" class vowels

| Mark | Name Vowel | Sound | Trans. | Class |
|---|---|---|---|---|
| ◌ | Chireq | "ee" as in green | i | Short |
| ◌ | Chireq Yod | "i" as in ski | i | Long |

## The "O" class vowels

| Mark | Name Vowel | Sound | Trans. | Class |
|---|---|---|---|---|
| ◌ | Cholem | "o" as in moses | o | Long |
| ◌ | Chateph Qamets | "o" as in whole | o | Reduced |
| ◌ | QametsChateph | "o" as in cone | o | Short |
| ◌ | Cholem Vav | "o" as in bow | o | Long |

| The "U" class vowels | | | | |
|---|---|---|---|---|
| **Mark** | **Name Vowel** | **Sound** | **Trans.** | **Class** |
| ◌ | Qibbuts | "oo" as in blue | u | Short |
| ◌ | Shureq | "oo" as in pool | u | Long |

| Sheva' | | | | |
|---|---|---|---|---|
| **Mark** | **Name Vowel** | **Sound** | **Trans.** | **Class** |
| ◌ | Sheva' | Vocal : Short "e" <br> Silent: no sound | e or ' | (Vocal) Short |

## How Hebrew Vowel Signs Work

vowels never appears on its own it is always connected to a letter

The signs are placed under the letters.
Just add the sound of the letter (which is a consonant) with the sound of the vowel and form the syllables.

## Example

the letter "Nun", which sounds like N,

added to the vowel A, which is a dash below the letter,
looks like this:

This syllable we pronounce NA
(with the "A" same as in "father").

If we put the vowel E, which are two dots below the letter,
it looks like this:

This syllable we pronounce NE
(with the "E" same as in "pen").

And so on … we can put any vowel for each letter.

Two letters of the alphabet can make vowel paper:
The letter Vav ו, and the letter Yod י.

Vav                          Yod

The vav with the dot at the top has the sound
of "O" as in "yellow",and the vav with the dot
at the bottom has the sound of "U" as in "blue".
And the letter Yod has the sound of "I" and in "green".

NO              NU              NI

These signs have remained to this day,
and they are what enables anyone to learn to read Hebrew.

## Vowels Practice

Write the vowel under the consonant letters. Pronounce each vowel sound as you write.
Some consonants (Aleph & ayin) have no sound but "carry" the vowel sound.
Remember to write from right to left.

### The "E" class vowels

| "ey" Long | "ei" Long | "e" Reduced | "e" short | "e/ei" Long |
|---|---|---|---|---|
| יֶ | יֵ | ֱ | ֶ | ֵ |

### The "A" class vowels

| "ah" Long | "a" Reduced | "a" short | "a" Long |
|---|---|---|---|
| הָ | ֲ | ַ | ָ |

אָ אָ אֲ אַ אַ

בּ

ג

ד

ח

ו

וּ

ח

צ

ר

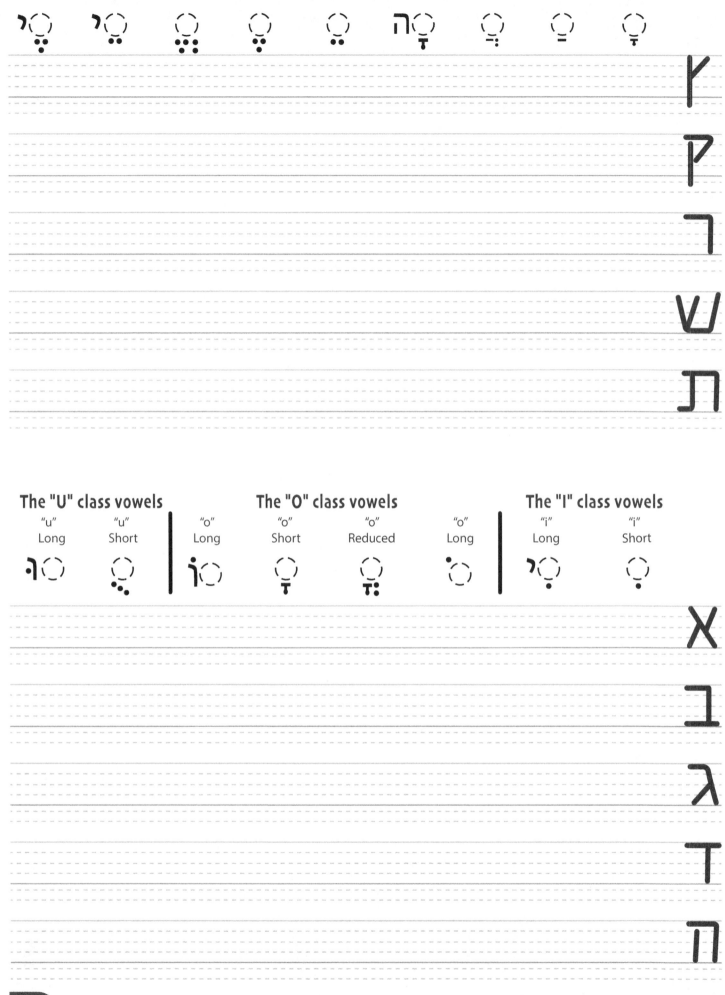

## The "U" class vowels

| "u" Long | "u" Short | | "o" Long |
|---|---|---|---|

## The "O" class vowels

| "o" Short | "o" Reduced | | "o" Long |
|---|---|---|---|

## The "I" class vowels

| "i" Long | "i" Short |
|---|---|

Made in the USA
Las Vegas, NV
07 January 2024

83994149R10070